PERIL FROM THE STARS

Earth has been invaded by the powerful robots from the distant planet Cybertron – the Heroic Autobots and their enemies, the Evil Decepticons. They can disguise their robot shapes as earthly machines and transform for battle at lightning speed. The battle between Good and Evil rages on Earth . . .

Also published by Young Corgi Books

THE TRANSFORMERS™: DINOBOT WAR
by Dave Morris

THE TRANSFORMERS™

ADVENTURE GAME BOOKS

Peril from the Stars

Dave Morris

Illustrated by Bob Harvey

YOUNG CORGI BOOKS

THE TRANSFORMERS™: PERIL FROM THE STARS

A YOUNG CORGI BOOK 0 552 523151

First publication in Great Britain.

PRINTING HISTORY

Young Corgi edition published 1985

Young Corgi Books are published by Transworld Publishers Ltd., 61–63 Uxbridge Road, Ealing, London W5 5SA.

Made and printed in Great Britain by the Guernsey Press Co. Ltd., Guernsey, Channel Islands.

This is an adventure story. But it is not like most other adventure stories – there is one big difference.

You are the main character.

What happens in the story depends on **your** decisions. The fate of The Transformers – whether the valiant JAZZ will prevail or whether the evil schemes of STARSCREAM will defeat him – is in **your** hands.

Do not read the pages of this adventure in numerical order, as you would an ordinary book. You should start at page ***1***, of course, but where you go to from there will depend on what you choose to do.

Prepare yourself to meet The Transformers!

NOW TURN TO PAGE ***1*** *...*

Your uncle and aunt are astronomers – but not the sort of astronomers who just sit around calculating things. They are much more adventurous than that, and are always travelling to exotic corners of the globe to watch distant nebulae through some of the world's most powerful telescopes. Presently they are staying at the secluded Los Palmos observatory, high up in the mountains. You are lucky enough to be able to visit them there for a week, and you are looking forward to quite an unusual holiday.

Uncle Jack picks you up at the airport and you begin the long drive up into the mountains. Uncle Jack seems to be absorbed with some problem or other, for he is puffing furiously at his pipe as he often does when he is thinking hard. After a while you stop at a petrol station, and Uncle Jack has just gone inside to pay the attendant when you see a brilliant flare of red light in the sky.

*If you tell Uncle Jack about the light, turn to page **2***
*If you decide to keep quiet about what you saw, turn to page **60***

A look of alarm appears on your uncle's face as you describe what you saw. You were not really sure that he would believe you, but he seems to be taking it all very seriously.

He is very worried that your aunt may be in danger. 'I'm going on up to the observatory,' he tells you as he jumps back into the car. 'You'd better stay here for now, and I'll come back and get you when I've checked things out up there.'

Uncle Jack calls out to Olaf, the big man who runs the petrol station, to take care of you for an hour or so. 'Sure thing, Dr Richards,' replies Olaf, wiping his hands on an oil rag. 'The kid'll be safe here.'

You watch your uncle drive off. Olaf tells you not to worry. 'You probably just saw an electrical storm or something,' he says but you know that Uncle Jack thought it was more than that. Olaf gets you a Coke from the fridge and then goes off to do some repairs to his truck.

If you wait here as your uncle asked you to, turn to page ***3***

If you sneak off and start walking up to the observatory, turn to page ***5***

Hours pass. The afternoon sun is hot and after a while Olaf gives up the work on his truck and comes out to doze on the porch. You hear a car approaching from further down the valley and you run out to see who is coming.

You are astonished to see a sleek white Porsche drawing up. Why are you astonished? Because it has no driver!

If you think you had better wake Olaf, turn to page **4**
If you get into the strange car, turn to page **7**

Olaf is slumped in his chair snoozing. You grab his arm and shake him, but he is such a sound sleeper that he just snores all the louder. Seeing that you cannot wake him, you abandon the attempt. You could never make him believe that a car drove here with no-one at the wheel, anyway. You are not sure that you believe it yourself! You go over and take another look.

Turn to page ***6***

A car is approaching from further down the valley. You have not walked very far, but it seems miles in the scorching mid-afternoon heat. A gleaming white Porsche pulls up beside you. You glance around, expecting to see a friendly face offering you a welcome lift – but there is no driver!

Turn to page **6**

Your astonishment grows even more when, a few moments later, a voice comes from the car: 'Better get in, kid. Things are going to be hotting up around here pretty soon!'

'Okay, that's it,' you call out angrily. 'I know there's someone in there. This is a lousy joke, if you ask me.'

'Joke? This is no joke,' says the voice again. 'I don't imagine there's anyone hiding inside *you*, so why should you suppose there's anyone inside me? Come on, open the door and take a look for yourself.'

You reach out and open the car door. Sure enough, there is no-one inside.

Turn to page **7**

'Really, you'd better hurry. We may not have much time.' The voice comes from a microphone set into the dashboard. You realize that the car itself is alive and talking to you.

'You look like a fish with your mouth gaping,' says the car. 'Hurry, hurry, hurry. You can be astonished once we're on our way.'

Noting the urgency in the voice, you climb in. As soon as you close the door, the car starts of its own accord and sets off on the winding road that leads to the observatory.

'Want some jive while we drive?' asks the car. Before you can reply, concealed stereo speakers launch into a swinging rhythm.

'Would you mind telling me who you are?' you yell, struggling to make yourself heard above the music.

The volume drops to a more comfortable level. 'Sorry – I didn't mean to deafen you. I'm JAZZ, one of The Transformers. I'm on a special mission for OPTIMUS PRIME. So are you, now, in a manner of speaking.'

You are about to pour out a torrent of questions when the great dome of the observatory comes into view, looming high on a crag ahead. Uncle Jack's car is stationary in the middle of the road. The door is open and you can see no sign of your uncle.

*If you get JAZZ to pull up here, turn to page **8***

*If you urge him to carry on to the observatory, turn to page **52***

'Hey, wait!' you yell suddenly. 'Something's wrong here. That's my uncle's car!'

JAZZ screeches to a halt just a few metres short of your uncle's abandoned car. 'Could be a trap,' he agrees. 'I'd better scan the area.'

Coloured lights wink on the dashboard as JAZZ's sensors play across your surroundings. 'Ah, yes,' remarks JAZZ suddenly. 'It's a good thing you stopped me when you did – we were about to drive straight into a null-field. That must be what stopped your uncle's car.'

You are about to ask JAZZ what a null-field is, but you decide you probably wouldn't understand the answer. The door opens next to you. 'You'll have to get out now. I must shield my circuits from the null-field, and for that I must get changed . . . '

'Changed into what?' you ask as you get out of the car. When you look back at JAZZ you can hardly believe your own eyes. At first it looks as though he is rearing up on his back wheels – then a robotic head appears from the hood of the Porsche, and mighty arms unfold from his sides. In moments he has become a mighty robot warrior standing on the dusty mountain road beside you!

*Turn to page **9***

'This is my true form,' JAZZ explains as he stoops to examine the abandoned car. 'We Autobots – like the Evil Decepticons – possess the ability to disguise ourselves as Earth-type machines. Luckily,' he adds, 'my own Earth-mode is one of the most stylish!'

Your uncle is not in the car or anywhere nearby. You assume that he went on to the observatory on foot when the mysterious null-field immobilized his car. JAZZ has come to the same conclusion. 'Perhaps you should wait here,' he suggests, 'while I investigate the observatory . . . '

If you go along with this plan, turn to page ***59***
If you insist on accompanying JAZZ, turn to page ***11***

JAZZ seems almost to shrug his armoured shoulders. 'Very well,' he says, 'it's up to you. But make sure you stay near me.' He reveals a bizarre rifle that shimmers in the bright sunlight.

'What could have caused the null-field?' you ask as you plod along the road to the observatory.

'I cannot be sure,' JAZZ replies, 'but I have a nasty suspicion that it has something to do with a very powerful foe of mine. Still, perhaps I am just being too cautious – it may be nothing so serious after all.'

Something catches your eye – a furtive movement behind a nearby boulder. JAZZ is preoccupied with keeping his sensors shielded from the null-field, and does not notice anything until you point it out.

If you want JAZZ to blast the boulder with his photon rifle, turn to page ***15***

If you wait to see who – or what – is behind the boulder, turn to page ***12***

Just as you draw level with the boulder, Uncle Jack steps out from behind it and stands in the road ahead of you. He has a revolver in his hand.

'Okay, robot,' he says to JAZZ. 'Better let the youngster go.' He waves the gun menacingly.

'To use an Earth-expression, you have got hold of the wrong end of the stick,' JAZZ replies. 'The youngster is my friend, not my captive,'

You are moving towards Uncle Jack. He sees that you are safe and begins to level the revolver at JAZZ. He is not sure whether to trust the robot or not. Suddenly a determined look appears on his face and you are sure he is about to fire.

If you knock his arm aside to spoil his aim, turn to page ***14***

If you stand by and let him shoot, turn to page ***16***

'No, Uncle Jack!' you shout as you push his arm aside. 'JAZZ is here to help us.'

The hastily-fired bullet misses your friend and throws a shower of rock fragments from a boulder behind him. Uncle Jack lowers the gun. 'I'm sorry, uh, JAZZ. Perhaps I'm too confused to think clearly – some strange things have been going on around here.'

'I know,' says JAZZ. 'That's why I have come. Let's go up to the observatory, and I'll explain everything.'

Turn to page ***22***

A narrow beam of searing light streams from the uncanny weapon and blasts the boulder into a hundred pieces. As you suspected, someone had been hiding behind it. One of the flying chunks of rock strikes him on the head and he falls with a groan.

'Look,' you say as you approach the unconscious man, 'he was armed.'

'So he was,' replies JAZZ, scooping up the revolver the man dropped. 'Let's take a look at him . . . '

JAZZ bends down and turns the man over with no effort. You get a real shock when you see his face. It's Uncle Jack!

Turn to page ***17***

You have already guessed that it would take more than a simple handgun to damage JAZZ with his powerful armour-planting, and you right. There is a metallic *clang* as the bullet ricochets off the Autobot, but his gleaming paintwork is not even scratched.

Suddenly Uncle Jack moans and falls down in the road. You turn to see that the bullet grazed his forehead when it rebounded off JAZZ. Both you and JAZZ are by his side in a moment. He is unconscious, but fortunately not badly hurt.

Turn to page ***17***

JAZZ easily lifts your uncle in his mighty arms, and you set off towards the observatory once more. As you approach, a slender figure emerges from the doorway and hurries towards you. You soon see that it is your Aunt Sue.

'What happened to Jack?' she cries out breathlessly. After a brief glance at JAZZ she turns to you. 'He went out to find you. Are you all right?'

'May I interrupt?' says JAZZ. 'Your husband is not badly damaged, ma'am – just a slight accident. I believe we should get him into the shade. I know you Earth people find heat uncomfortable.'

JAZZ lumbers up to the observatory and stoops to get through the door. You and your aunt quickly follow him inside.

*Turn to page **19***

JAZZ places your uncle's unconscious body on a couch. For all his great strength and fearsome weaponry, you notice that the giant robot is very gentle. Looking pale and drawn, your aunt scurries away and returns shortly with a damp cloth which she places on Uncle Jack's forehead. Only when she has cleaned and finished dressing his wound does she turn to you and JAZZ.

'I don't understand what's going on around here,' she says. 'First all the electrical equipment goes haywire, then a robot turns up on the doorstep!'

JAZZ bows, 'Ah, I have neglected to introduce myself. I am JAZZ, Special Operative for the Heroic Autobots. As for my purpose in coming here – perhaps I should save that explanation until your husband comes round. For now, I think I shall take a look around.'

He goes outside again.

*If you follow JAZZ, turn to page **20***

*If you stay in the observatory with your aunt and uncle, turn to page **21***

'Hey, wait for me,' you shout, running to catch up with your Autobot friend. 'I don't know what we're looking around for, but there's more chance of finding it if two of us look!'

'Logical,' admits JAZZ. 'I am hoping to find the device that powers the null-field – or one of them, at least, for there are probably several in the vicinity.'

'That's what knocked out Uncle Jack's car, right? Why would anyone set up devices to do that?'

JAZZ is clambering up a nearby rock outcropping. He seems tireless, but you are soon panting with the effort of keeping up. 'Someone wants to prevent you from interfering with their evil plan, and I have a feeling I know who that someone is . . . '

His voice trails off and he points to a small metal box some distance away. 'There – one of the null-field generators. I can go no closer without risking damage to my more delicate sensory circuits.'

It is up to you.

If you throw a rock to smash the device, turn to page ***23***

If you walk over and disconnect it, turn to page ***24***

You watch JAZZ searching around the observatory, but he does not seem to be having any success.

'Ohhh, my head!' You turn to see your uncle sitting up – thankfully, it seems he was not badly hurt. Aunt Sue flings her arms around him. Outside it is starting to get dark.

'What happened?' says Uncle Jack, still slightly dazed. He looks at you. 'I had some dream – I thought I saw you with a giant robot!'

A bulky shape appears in the doorway. 'Uh, that was no dream, Uncle Jack,' you reply. 'This is my friend JAZZ.'

Uncle Jack looks dumbfounded as JAZZ shakes hands with him. 'Please do not be alarmed, sir. I'm here to help – let's go up to the dome, and I'll try to explain what's going on,'

Turn to page ***26***

The three of you set off towards the observatory. As you approach, you see the slim figure of your aunt emerge and come hurrying towards you.

'Sue!' your uncle calls out to her. 'This is JAZZ, and he says he's a friend.'

Aunt Sue watches JAZZ suspiciously, but then she smiles at you and ruffles your hair. 'I'm glad to see you're okay. Come on inside now – it will be getting dark soon.'

Sure enough, the sun is already dipping below the horizon. You can feel the chill of night in the air. As you enter the observatory, JAZZ suggests that you all go up to the dome. He is going to explain his mission to you.

Turn to page ***26***

The first couple of rocks you try throwing fall wide of the mark, but the third is right on target. There is a satisfying crunch as it lands on the null-field device and a wisp of smoke curls up from the severed wires and smashed circuit boards.

'Well done,' says JAZZ. He goes over and crushes the box with an earth-shaking stamp of his enormous metal foot. 'This is one device that will never serve the purposes of the Evil Decepticons again.'

Turn to page ***25***

JAZZ is about to blow the device up with his photon rifle, but you have a better idea. Scrambling down to where it lies half-concealed beside a rock, you examine it more closely. Its energy-scrambling rays present some danger to JAZZ with his electrical senses, but cannot harm you.

You see that a wire connects the device's power-pack to the aerial which is emitting the null-rays. It is a simple task to pull the wire out, and once you have done this the device is harmless. You tuck it under your arm and carry it back to show to JAZZ.

'It is inactive now,' he says, congratulating you. 'Why not keep it? We may even find a way to turn it against its evil master . . . '

Turn to page ***25***

It is now late in the afternoon, and night falls quickly in this part of the world. JAZZ picks you up and puts you on his shoulder. He wants to get back to the observatory without delay.

'Something that struck me as odd,' he murmurs on the way back, 'was the way your aunt wasn't surprised when she first saw me. She can't be used to robot visitors, surely?'

All you can suggest is that she was too worried about your uncle to think of anything else. It is almost dark by the time you reach the observatory. JAZZ sets you down. Entering, you are delighted to see that Uncle Jack has recovered consciousness. Except for a bandage around his head, he looks none the worse for wear.

'Sorry,' he says to JAZZ. 'Things have been a bit odd around here recently, and when I saw you I jumped to the conclusion that you were an enemy.'

'Why don't we go up to the dome,' suggests JAZZ. 'I'll tell you who the *real* enemy is.'

*Turn to page **26***

A spiral staircase leads up into the vast dome of the observatory. As you reach the top, the first thing you see is the telescope itself. It is vast – perhaps fifteen metres long, and surrounded by the computer-operated hydraulic supports that can direct it to any specified point in the heavens.

JAZZ turns to your uncle. 'Doctor Richards, can you tell me of any strange incidents to have occurred around here recently?'

Uncle Jack takes out his pipe. 'Well, the first thing was when we were observing the Farouki cluster late last night. There was a brilliant burst of red light in the sky and the instruments all went haywire for several minutes. A similar phenomenon occurred this morning, just as I was about to set off for the airport. And as you know, the ignition on my car failed on the way back here this afternoon.'

'It is as I suspected,' says JAZZ solemnly, nodding his head. 'All the evidence points to one of the deadliest Decepticons of them all – '

The name hangs in the air like a death-knell: ' – STARSCREAM.'

*Turn to page **28***

With night falling outside the dome, the three of you listen attentively as JAZZ tells his story:

'The Transformers came originally from the planet Cybertron. One group of us – the Autobots, the group to which I belong – are peace-loving and mean no harm to the people of Earth. But the other group, the Evil Decepticons, delight only in conquest and destruction.

'Recently, while studying our ancient records, I discovered that a space pod containing many powerful weapons was launched from Cybertron when our planet passed close to your own. This happened many millions of years ago, and the pod must have been drifting in orbit around your sun since then. Obviously, STARSCREAM has also learned of these weapons and hopes to acquire them.'

If you ask JAZZ for more information about STARSCREAM, turn to page ***29***

If you ask him why he thinks STARSCREAM is interested in the observatory, turn to page ***30***

'STARSCREAM is one of the most powerful of the Decepticons, and for sheer cruelty he has no equal. He can transform himself into a supersonic fighter plane and is armed with powerful cluster bombs and disruptive null-rays. I am sure that the failure of electrical apparatus here yesterday was due to STARSCREAM's arrival. Since the equipment in the observatory – ' JAZZ gestures at the winking banks of computer displays – 'is now working perfectly, he has obviously set up his null-field devices pointing outwards from this location.'

'So that if the authorities get wind of what he's up to, any attack they launch will be immobilized before it gets here,' says Uncle Jack.

'Just as your car was, precisely. Now, pardon me,' says JAZZ. 'I must spend the next few minutes considering the possible ways in which STARSCREAM may choose to act now.' He bows his head, deep in thought.

Turn to page ***32***

'STARSCREAM needs a powerful telescope to locate the weapons pod in space,' replies your Autobot friend. 'He could not use the telescopes and computers at Decepticon HQ, because that would alert his fellow Decepticons to his plan. Treacherous STARSCREAM is forever plotting to take over from mighty MEGATRON as leader of the evil forces. If the weapons pod falls into his hands, he may well succeed!'

The thought of that makes you shudder. JAZZ tells you that he must spend a few minutes analyzing the enemy's probable courses of action. He bows his head, deep in thought.

*Turn to page **32***

JAZZ suddenly says, 'Perhaps you would like to be entertained by some excellent Earth music?' Loud orchestral music blares from JAZZ's built-in speakers and echoes around the huge dome.

'Hey – yeeow! Turn it down, JAZZ,' you tell him. Uncle Jack covers his ears. Aunt Sue does not seem to be bothered by the noise.

'Sorry,' JAZZ says to you, 'I keep forgetting you Earth people can't tolerate the same level of noise that we Transformers can. My speakers can reach 180 decibels, you know,' he remarks proudly.

'Just so long as we're nowhere nearby when they do!' says your uncle, chuckling.

Suddenly everyone goes quiet. JAZZ stops the music. Straining your ears, you hear the sound of an aeroplane approaching the observatory.

Turn to page ***33***

'That's STARSCREAM.' murmurs JAZZ, listening to the drone of the aircraft's engines. 'But why is he coming in at subsonic speed . . . ?'

You think you can hear a second set of engines along with the first. 'Maybe he's going slowly so that a slower Decepticon can keep up?' you suggest.

JAZZ nods slowly. 'Yes, it all fits. You see, I've noticed that your aunt has been behaving very strangely for an Earth person . . . '

You all look round to discover Aunt Sue holding a gun on you. 'Sue!' exclaims Uncle Jack.

'She is under the control of BOMBSHELL, another Decepticon,' says JAZZ. 'He must have attacked the observatory this afternoon, when she was alone here, and implanted one of his cerebro-shells into her head. He is beaming radio signals to tell her what to do!'

'Put your weapons down, Autobot,' Aunt Sue says dully 'or I will shoot Jack.'

If you have the deactivated null-field device, turn to page ***35***

If you do not have this device, turn to page ***36***

Under the control of the vile BOMBSHELL,your aunt is almost like a sleepwalker. She does not notice when you take the null-field generator from your pocket and reconnect the aerial. You direct its electricity-disrupting rays at her head, and she suddenly seems to come out of a trance. 'What's going on?' she asks, lowering the gun.

The aircraft engines are drawing nearer.

'Quickly,' says JAZZ. 'The null-rays have blocked BOMBSHELLS's control signals. We must remove the cerebro-shell.' He steps close to your aunt and lifts up her hair. There is a small bump on the side of her head, just behind her ear, where BOMBSHELL implanted his cerebro-shell below the skin. JAZZ adjusts his photon rifle to get a pencil thin beam and uses it to remove the cerebro-shell. Your aunt barely feels a thing.

'Yukk!' she says, looking at the cerebro-shell before handing it to you. 'Fancy having something like that in my head! I've been under BOMBSHELL's control since this morning, but I couldn't tell you. It felt as if I was sleepwalking.'

'Listen!' interrupts JAZZ. 'The sound of STAR-SCREAM's engines has stopped – '

*Turn to page **37***

There is a blinding pulse of light from JAZZ and everyone shields their eyes. Taking advantage of your aunt's confusion, JAZZ steps forward and seizes her before she can pull the trigger. She struggles, but cannot get free of the Autobot's metallic grasp. When he pushes her hair back, you see BOMBSHELL's implant as a bump under the skin behind her ear.

Using a narrow laser beam from his rifle as deftly as a surgeon might use a scalpel, JAZZ removes the cerebro-shell and crushes it underfoot. Aunt Sue staggers over to your uncle. 'Thank goodness I'm rid of that ghastly device. I've been under BOMBSHELL's control for hours. If not for JAZZ, I might have killed you all!'

Outside, the scream of STARSCREAM's jets builds before cutting out. You can now hear only the low hum of BOMBSHELL's engines approaching.

*Turn to page **37***

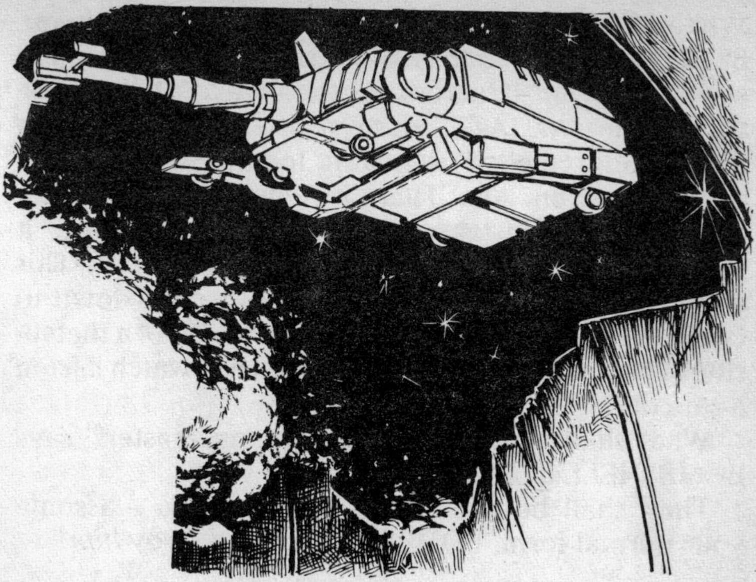

'STARSCREAM's gone to supersonic speed,' realizes JAZZ. 'Everyone – get down!'

As you throw yourselves to the floor, one side of the dome explodes into fragments of stone and twisted steel. Through the broken gap you can see the starry night sky. A powerful fighter plane sweeps in and drops towards the floor of the dome, transforming into the forbidding figure of STARSCREAM. A loud rumbling in the sky follows him like a thunderclap – because of his supersonic velocity, he got here before the sound of his jets did.

A horrible blue shape hangs in the air above the dome and then starts to descend. It looks like a giant insect. BOMBSHELL prefers to remain in his Insecticon form for now – he knows that it frightens you.

*Turn to page **38***

While BOMBSHELL keeps an eye on the four of you, STARSCREAM marches over to the telescope and starts to swing it across the heavens. 'As I'm sure you've guessed, JAZZ,' he says with a note of triumph in his tinny voice, 'I'm looking for the weapons pod from Cybertron. Aha! There it is, floating close to the asteroid belt.' He takes out a small metal sphere. It starts to bleep when he presses a stud on the side. 'This is a homing beacon which will call the pod down to Earth. It will fall with the destructive power of a meteorite, of course, so BOMBSHELL and I shall watch it from a safe distance.'

'What shall we do with the humans, master?' says BOMBSHELL in a creepy humming voice.

'They shall be our slaves. As for JAZZ – assume your normal form, BOMBSHELL, *and destroy him*!'

If you have the cerebro-shell that was controlling your aunt, turn to page ***39***

If you do not have that device, turn to page ***41***

BOMBSHELL takes little notice of you humans – all his attention is on JAZZ. As he transforms into his robot-form, you throw the cerebro-shell so that it lodges into the armour at the back of his neck. 'Take care!' STARSCREAM warns. 'The small human threw something at you.'

BOMBSHELL would rather fight humans than the powerful JAZZ. He turns towards you. 'Humans are no problem,' he snarls. 'I can make them my puppets with the cerebro-shells.' He activates his controlling signal.

*Turn to page **42***

JAZZ lifts his photon rifle as BOMBSHELL moves towards him. BOMBSHELL seems uneasy; his step falters. 'Will you not assist me, mighty STARSCREAM?' he whines.

'Bah! Are you afraid of JAZZ? He is hardly the strongest of the Autobots.' STARSCREAM also moves towards your friend. JAZZ seems uncertain what to do – then suddenly he jumps backwards and presses a button on a panel behind him. It is the button that controls the telescope's movements. The huge telescope rotates quickly and descends on to BOMBSHELL. Its hydraulic supports pin the foul Insecticon to the floor.

Turn to page ***43***

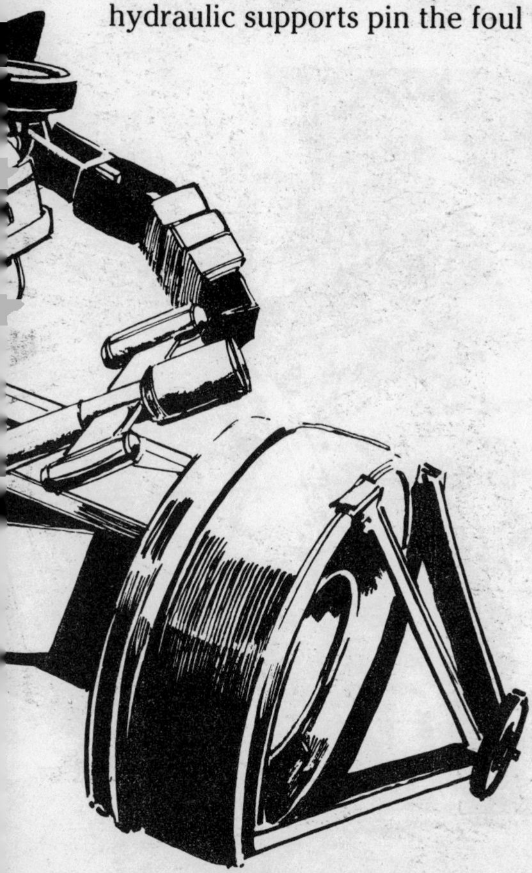

Having primed his cerebro-shells, BOMBSHELL lurches towards you. He intends to inject his devices into your heads and turn you into his slaves. But the cerebro-shell which you threw at him is also activated now. It starts to give off confusing messages. The effect is like feedback on a stereo system, and BOMBSHELL starts to wave his arms wildly. JAZZ adds to the Insecticon's troubles with a steady burst of high-frequency noise from his speakers. Terrified, BOMBSHELL turns back into his insect-form and scuttles away.

*Turn to page **43***

STARSCREAM glances up into the sky. Following his gaze, you see a tiny pinprick of light – it must be the weapons pod entering the Earth's atmosphere. JAZZ starts to bring his flame thrower to bear on the two Decepticons, but before he can do so STARSCREAM unleashes a concussive blast which stuns him.

'Farewell, humans,' rages STARSCREAM as he begins to resume his aircraft-form. 'I must depart before the weapons pod smashes this place to rubble.'

His mechanical laughter is drowned out by the roar as his jets ignite. You look to JAZZ, but he is still too groggy to act. STARSCREAM's homing beacon, which is attracting the falling weapons pod straight towards it, lies on the floor beside the telescope.

If you want to get the homing beacon and hurl it at STARSCREAM, turn to page ***44***

If you want to put it in your pocket, turn to page ***46***

You run across to the flashing beacon, snatch it up, and throw it. Luck is with you – the beacon, drops into the air intake on one of STARSCREAM's jets and catches there. To the over-confident Decepticon, you are too insignificant to matter, and so he fails to notice what you have done.

With a thundering roar, STARSCREAM speeds up away from the dome. The weapons pod is descending fast, and it swerves in the air to follow him.

STARSCREAM does not realize that this is because the beacon is lodged inside his jet, and he is too astonished to dodge. The heavy pod smashes through his starboard wing like a shooting star! Thick black clouds bellow from STARSCREAM's broken wing. Any normal plane would drop from the sky, but he is a master of flying and somehow manages to glide away.

Turn to page ***47***

You slip the flashing beacon into your pocket as STARSCREAM roars up away from the dome. BOMBSHELL has also recovered now, and he quickly flies after his master. Your uncle and aunt are standing around, dazed with shock, as JAZZ searches frantically for something amid the debris.

*If you tell JAZZ you have the homing beacon, turn to page **50***

*If you keep quiet about it, turn to page **51***

JAZZ steps towards BOMBSHELL, who has now recovered. 'It seems that your evil master is running away,' laughs the Autobot as he raises his flame thrower. 'Are you prepared to continue our battle alone, Insecticon?'

BOMBSHELL's eyes sparkle with alarm. He has no wish to stay and fight JAZZ on his own, so he rapidly soars aloft and speeds off behind his damaged master.

*Turn to page **68***

Two giant robots stand beside the observatory. The larger of them is herding your uncle and aunt inside. They are too far away for you to hear what is being said, but you can tell from the robots' swaggering stance and the way that Uncle Jack is shaking his fist that they are up to no good.

JAZZ soon confirms what you have already realized. 'This is bad news,' he says. 'Those two are STARSCREAM and BOMBSHELL – members of the Evil Decepticons. Since I can't change to my own robot-form, I would have difficulty fighting them both.'

If you suggest that JAZZ rams BOMBSHELL once the larger robot is out of sight, turn to page ***53***

If you think it would be better to drive off, turn to page ***55***

JAZZ holds out his hand. 'Quickly, give it to me.'

You hand him the flashing beacon. The weapons pod, which is now visible like a comet in the night sky, is falling straight towards it. JAZZ smashes the beacon in the palm of his steel-shod hand. With its homing beacon destroyed, the fallings weapons pod spins out of control and screeches overhead

'I estimate it will come down in the Pacific Ocean. A fitting place for those deadly weapons, for STAR-SCREAM will never find them there.'

*Turn to page **68***

Too bad you don't mention that you have the homing beacon, because that is exactly what JAZZ is so anxious to find. The descending weapons pod is heading straight towards it! It will hit the ground exactly where you are standing, and the impact will destroy the observatory – to say nothing of its human occupants. Best that we close the book on this dreadful scene, for this is

THE END

'Yeeowwww!' shouts JAZZ as he drives past your uncle's abandoned car. Sparks sizzle wildly across his dashboard. He swerves, then keeps on going. There is a smell of burnt-out wiring in the car.

'What happened?' you ask.

'We drove straight into a null-field. It scrambles electrical energy – must be what knocked out the ignition on your uncle's car. Stupid of me not to have guessed that. It's burned out some vital circuitry, and now I can't switch to my robot-mode.'

Before you can ask him what he means by that, you see something up ahead that drives all other thoughts from your head.

*Turn to page **48***

JAZZ is enthusiastic about the plan. As soon as STARSCREAM has taken your aunt and uncle inside, he shifts gears and screeches along the dusty road towards BOMBSHELL. The Decepticon starts to turn, but he is too late to avoid JAZZ's attack. The Porsche's fender smashes into him, buckling one of his metal legs.

'That's damaged his wing case,' yells JAZZ enthusiastically. 'Now it's time for us to make a temporary retreat.' He goes into reverse and speeds off back along the road, dodging several explosive salvos from the damaged BOMBSHELL.

*Turn to page **58***

Even with your fingers in your ears, you can hear the piercing wail coming from JAZZ's loudspeakers. Olaf jumps up out of his chair as though he had been pricked with a pin. 'Yipes! What was that – ?' he cries. You cannot help laughing.

It is not easy to convince Olaf that the Porsche parked outside his garage is actually a transformed robot. Only when he has peered underneath, looked under the seats and opened the bonnet does he accept it. 'Well, I never saw wiring like this in any car I ever overhauled!' he exclaims as he scratches the back of his head.

'Can you take a look and see if you can see any burned-out connections?' asks JAZZ. 'The circuits that allow me to assume my robot-form are broken.'

Olaf fetches his tools and rummages around under the bonnet for several minutes. As he stands back at last, there is a whirring noise from JAZZ. Suddenly, the Porsche's chassis begins to rearrange and reform. Before you have time to take in take in what is happening, JAZZ has changed from his car-form into a giant white robot warrior!

*Turn to page **62***

JAZZ dislikes the idea of running away, but he knows that it is wise to get himself repaired before taking on his enemies. With his motor purring quietly, he starts to reverse down the road away from the observatory.

Unfortunately, BOMBSHELL is alert and notices you. Yelling out to warn STARSCREAM, he leaps into the air and transforms to become a hideous blue beetle. Moments later, he is speeding after you in hot pursuit.

If you think JAZZ should try to outrun him, turn to page ***57***

If you get JAZZ to stop right now, turn to page ***56***

JAZZ throws on the brakes as you suggest. The Porsche screeches to a halt, and you smell the rubber of the tyres as they skid on the hot mountain road. Luckily, your ploy works – BOMBSHELL cannot turn very quickly in the air, so he overshoots and comes to rest hovering some distance ahead of you.

'I've got him square in my sights!' whoops JAZZ gleefully. A lance of laser-light stabs up from his headlights and sends a spray of molten metal through BOMBSHELL's wing-case. As the Decepticon drops, unable to stay in the air with his wing damaged, JAZZ speeds off down the hill.

Turn to page ***58***

Up in the air, BOMBSHELL easily overtakes the Porsche. He swings like a blue-black angel of death and alights on a crag. As he switches to robot-form, a powerful mortar tilts from his head. JAZZ brakes wildly, but he is too late. An explosive shell spits from the Decepticon's deadly mortar, and for you and JAZZ this is

THE END

'Luck's been with us so far,' says JAZZ. 'I could never hope to beat STARSCREAM in this form, but it seems he isn't intending to pursue us anyway.'

'I don't know much about all this,' you reply, 'but I can see that you're the good guy – and that those other two robots will hurt my uncle and aunt if we don't stop them. Why not drive back to the petrol station – Olaf's quite a mechanic, and he might be able to patch you up.'

JAZZ agrees that this is a good plan, and you are soon back at the petrol station. Olaf is dozing in the shade. You leap out of the Porsche and try to shake him awake, but you have no success – he sleeps too soundly.

'Let me try,' says JAZZ. 'Better cover your ears – '

Turn to page ***54***

Nervously, you wait beside the abandoned car as JAZZ lumbers off towards the observatory. You watch until he has turned a corner out of sight. You cannot guess what mission has brought the Autobot warrior to this secluded place, but you are certainly glad he has come. Perhaps he will be able to find Uncle Jack.

Sure enough, you have been waiting only a few minutes when JAZZ comes back. Uncle Jack is with him, and the two are chatting like old friends.

'Hope I didn't give you a fright, disappearing like that,' says your uncle with a grin. 'The car just stopped dead on me – JAZZ says I drove into something called a null-field.'

'I think,' says JAZZ, 'that we had better waste no time in getting up to the observatory.'

Turn to page ***22***

Uncle Jack gets back into the car and you drive on up towards the observatory. You watch the breathtaking mountain scenery fly by, but your uncle hardly notices it. Puffing on his pipe, he is miles away.

Suddenly the engine sputters and the car lurches to a halt. Uncle Jack tries the ignition, but it is dead. 'What on Earth – ?' he murmurs to himself.

At just that moment a sleek Porsche pulls up beside you. You and your uncle stand baffled – for there is no-one at the wheel!

*Turn to page **61***

'Are you having trouble?' inquires the Porsche. 'I'm JAZZ, one of the Autobots. I'd venture to say that your car has been immobilized by a null-field.'

Suddenly the Porsche's doors and hood unfold as it undergoes an incredible transformation. Within a few moments, it is no longer a car that stands beside you, but a tall robot warrior armed with powerful laser rifle.

JAZZ gestures at your uncle's car. 'I'm afraid I have to change to my robot-form to keep my circuits shielded from the null-field. We'll have to go the rest of the way to the observatory on foot.'

*Turn to page **22***

Olaf steps back in amazement. 'Well, I'll be – ' he says. 'What're you, a new model?'

JAZZ replies with a sound very like a human laugh. 'No. We Transformers have the ability to take on the outward appearance of certain Earth machines. Few are blessed with so stylish an Earth-form as my own! I thank you for repairing my damaged circuitry, human friend.'

'Hey,' you remind him. 'Don't forget that those other robots still have my aunt and uncle.'

JAZZ nods. He takes a few strides along the road to the observatory and you have to walk pretty quickly to keep up. Olaf shouts after you: 'That wiring I put in isn't much more than a patch-up job, Mr JAZZ. Try not to shift shape too often before you can get it rewired properly – you might burn out the circuit again.'

JAZZ waves his thanks as you continue up the road together. 'HOIST or RATCHET can make full repairs on my circuits when I return to the Ark – but there's no time for that now. Shall I switch to my vehicle-form, and risk getting stuck in that shape again – or shall I retain my robot-form, even though it will take longer to get up to the observatory?'

If you think JAZZ should play safe and stay in his robot-form, turn to page ***63***

If you suggest that he changes into the car again so that you can drive quickly up to the observatory, turn to page ***64***

With JAZZ at your side, you trudge along the sun-baked mountain road towards the observatory. It is not long before you are exhausted. There is no time to stop for a rest, so JAZZ perches you on his shoulder. Though he covers three metres with each stride, it is after nightfall when you finally reach the great dome of the observatory. You can hear voices inside. One is raised in ranting rage. It is the cold, mechanical voice of STARSCREAM.

*Turn to page **65***

JAZZ is reluctant to accept your suggestion at first. 'If I get stuck in car-form again, there is little chance of defeating STARSCREAM and BOMBSHELL.'

'But if you don't get us up there fast', you point out, 'we may be too late to save my uncle and aunt.'

JAZZ nods, and you watch as he swiftly alters his form to become the swift Porsche again. You hop in, and JAZZ roars up the winding road. He accelerates and manoeuvres more expertly than any human driver could, taking the sharp clifftop bends at breathtaking speed. As you near your uncle's abandoned car, he pulls up to let you get out. 'I must return to my robot-form now,' he explains, 'in order to shield my circuits from the null-field.' Again he becomes a towering metal warrior, and the two of you stride on towards the observatory.

Night is falling. From inside the dome, a ranting mechanical voice echoes out. It is the voice of STAR-SCREAM.

Turn to page ***65***

Through the lengthening shadows of dusk, you and JAZZ stalk closer to the dome. Sparkling stars are appearing in the sky, like a scattering of gems on a velvet cloth. You strain your ears to catch what is being said.

There is a man's voice – your uncle! 'STARSCREAM,' he says. 'What have you got to gain by holding us captive? Sooner or later we'll be missed, and then – '

'I have no interest at all in you puny humans!' snaps STARSCREAM. 'For millions of years, a weapons pod from the planet Cybertron – our home world – has orbited in your solar system. The Autobots and even my fellow Decepticons thought it lost forever, but with the aid of your telescope I have just located it. I mean to bring it down to Earth and use the weapons within it to rule over the entire human race – and over each and every Transformer battle robot as well!'

JAZZ turns to you. 'I guess I don't need to tell you that STARSCREAM is mad, do I?' he whispers. 'But his plan is only too real – we must stop him.'

*To see if you can, turn to page **66***

You enter the observatory and cautiously ascend the steps that lead into the dome. STARSCREAM stands beside the telescope. It is famed throughout the world for its size, one of the largest optical telescopes known – but it is barely bigger than the looming Decepticon. As soon as he sees you, he holds out a small metal sphere and presses a stud on the side of it. The sphere starts to bleep.

'You are too late to stop me, JAZZ,' he sneers. 'This homing beacon is now activated. It is sending signals up to the weapons pod that will cause it to leave its orbit and come hurtling down to Earth. But you will not survive to see that! BOMBSHELL – destroy him . . .'

BOMBSHELL, the Insecticon, is guarding your uncle and aunt. They seem frightened but unhurt, and call out when they see you.

BOMBSHELL moves towards JAZZ. Though he is limping from the damage to his wing-case (his leg, now that he is in his robot form) the mortar gun on his head looks terrifyingly powerful. However, JAZZ is prepared for him. Your Autobot friend creates a burst of blinding light and a blast of ultrasound that send BOMBSHELL staggering back in pain and confusion.

*Turn to page **43***

STARSCREAM's evil plan has been thwarted and your uncle and aunt are safe. Though the dome was shattered when STARSCREAM blasted his way through it, the damage can be repaired. Fortunately, the priceless telescope is not even scratched.

Though it is late, your uncle and aunt insist on asking JAZZ a stream of questions – about his home world, how he and The Transformers came to Earth, the strange technology they possess. You are almost overcome with wonder at JAZZ's incredible tales. When he finally leaves, it is almost dawn.

After saying goodbye to your friend, you stand with your uncle and aunt watching him drive away along the lonely mountain road. You know that he and his companions will continue the struggle against the Evil Decepticons. And if, as you hope, they ever win that struggle, a small step on the way to that victory will have been won with your help.

THE END

THE TRANSFORMERS DINOBOT WAR
by Dave Morris

Robot Dinosaurs!

Earth has been invaded by the powerful robots from the distant plant Cybertron – the Heroic Autobots and their enemies, the Evil Decepticons. They can disguise their robot shapes as earthly machines and transform for battle at lightning speed. The battle between Good and Evil rages on Earth . . .

You are the hero of this book – suddenly you are thrust into the deadly struggle. With the help of secret devices, found on an ancient flying saucer, you could travel back to prehistoric times and help the Heroic Dinobots in their battle against the Evil Decepticons.

If you dare . . .

If you collect Transformers™, this book is for you!

SBN 0 552 523143

T.R. BEAR: ENTER T.R.
by Terrance Dicks

It all started when Jimmy got a parcel from his Uncle Colin in America. The teddy bear inside was unlike any bear Jimmy had ever seen. He looked tough, and he was wearing glasses! According to the label, his name was Theodore Roosevelt, T.R. for short.

Jimmy soon found out that life with T.R. Bear was quite eventful . . .

SBN 0 552 523011

THE GOONIES™: CAVERN OF HORROR
by William Rotsler

The Goonies are here! Join that lovable gaggle of gangly kids in their quest for One-Eyed Willie's treasure as they face off against criminal forces, booby-trapped skeletons and the shrewd pirate's legacy of riddles, traps and surprises. Only *you* control the action! You lead the Goonies on their quest. Now, get ready to perform the secret Goonies' handshake, recite the Goony oath, and set out for adventure of goon-erific proportions . . . .

A Plot-it-yourself Adventure story based on Steven Spielberg's action-packed film.

SBN 0 552 523313

WIZARDS, WARRIORS & YOU™

A game of fantasy role-playing as well as a book.

In each adventure, you will choose to play the game as either the Wizard or the Warrior. Wearing the Wizard's robes, you will summon up magical spells to fend off your enemies. Carrying the Warrior's sword, you will use your strength and brilliance in battle to prevail against all challengers.

You must choose now – will you be the Wizard or the Warrior?

0 552 522821	THE FOREST OF TWISTED DREAMS
0 552 52283X	THE SIEGE OF THE DRAGONRIDERS
0 552 522848	WHO KIDNAPPED PRINCESS SARALINDA?
0 552 522864	GHOST KNIGHTS OF CAMELOT

WHICH WAY BOOKS

Your opportunity to join in the never-ending battles against the evil forces of the Universe!

WHICH WAY books bring to life your favourite characters of film and cartoon and *you* make the life-or-death decisions that guide each adventure to its close. Help *Superman* battle the evil *Phantom Zone villains*, join *Supergirl* as she fights the deadly dragons of King Arthur's England, control the fate of *The Justice League of America* as it battles crime and evil – or explore astounding new worlds on the Starship *Enterprise!* Remember – you control every adventure!

0 552 522562	SUPERMAN: MAN OF STEEL by Andrew Helfer
0 552 522589	SUPERGIRL: GIRL OF STEEL by Andrew Helfer
0 552 522570	JUSTICE LEAGUE OF AMERICA by Andrew Helfer
0 552 522716	STAR TREK® : VOYAGE TO ADVENTURE by Michael J Dodge

If you would like to receive a newsletter telling you about our new children's books, fill in the coupon with your name and address and send it to:

The Children's Books Editor,
Transworld Publishers Ltd.,
61–63 Uxbridge Road, Ealing,
London, W5 5SA

Name ....

Address ....

....

....

CHILDREN'S NEWSLETTER

All the books on the previous pages are available at your bookshop or can be ordered direct from Transworld Publishers Ltd., Cash Sales Dept., P.O. Box 11, Falmouth, Cornwall.
Please send full name and address together with cheque or postal order — no currency, and allow 55p per book to cover postage and packing (plus 22p each for additional copies).